THE SETTING

The site of Carisbrooke Castle is superb. Sweeping in from Newport is a long ridge which terminates abruptly, the land dropping away dramatically on three sides. The village of Carisbrooke is still attractive at its centre but is disfigured by suburban sprawl. However, to the south and west of the castle visitors today see almost exactly what the original builders would have seen nearly 1000 years ago: a wide shallow valley sweeping up to a clear skyline on which an advancing army would stand out. Winding round the foot of this great natural bastion is a small river, too shallow to provide defence but evidence that the site would provide the primary need of a medieval castle: water. This was a site almost custom built for a military engineer.

The first important reference to the castle was in 1136 when it was described as being

'*A stately castle built of hewn stone*'

but there is no other written evidence for its history until the thirteenth century and one has to rely on archaeological investigations to provide the story for its earliest period. Was there ever a Roman fort here? There was certainly a Roman villa barely a stone's throw away in what is now the outskirts of the village, and excavations in the castle in the 1920s and 1960s produced what seemed to be evidence of Roman origin. However, a more detailed excavation, carried out with improved archaeological techniques in the 1970s, disproved this theory.

Carisbrooke Castle is almost certainly of Saxon origin, one of the *burhs* or fortified camps thrown up to defend England against the Vikings. When the Normans, in their turn, looked for a good place on which to establish their own stronghold, they found that the stone-faced banks of the Saxon

The earliest known drawing of the castle (1567)

Newport Ligger Book

fortifications provided them with an excellent immediate defence urgently needed in the heart of a conquered resentful population. Their first castle cut off one corner of this enclosure. In due course they extended their ramparts over the Saxon defences and these banks exactly follow the line of the Saxon walls. One can still see traces of the original *burh* walls half buried on the east and west sides of the green banks.

He who held Carisbrooke held the Isle of Wight and the island was itself an ideal springboard for an attack on the mainland. From the beginning, therefore, the Crown had a close interest in the castle. William the Conqueror thought it so important that he gave it to his kinsman, William Fitzosbern, who began the task of turning the old Saxon *burh* into a Norman castle by building a campaign fort in one corner. He probably also built a great hall, the forerunner of the present building, for it was there that William the Conqueror arrested his own treacherous half-brother Odo in 1082 but there is now no trace of it.

As the years passed and the Crown became all powerful, so the King was able to exert ever more direct control on this vital bulwark of southern England. The Fitzosberns lost the castle after an unsuccessful rebellion in 1078 but their successors, the Norman family de Redvers, held it for nearly 200 years, from 1100 to 1293 and it was they who built much of the castle that one sees today. Probably the first Richard de Redvers threw up the existing motte and bailey [mound and courtyard], and the stone walls had been added to both by 1136. This enlargement of the castle was probably motivated by his desire to demonstrate his prestige as Lord of the Island. The last of the family was the Countess Isabella, and this formidable lady ruled the castle and the island for thirty years.

Isabella was only twenty-three when

Aerial view of the castle looking east

Isle of Wight Tourist Board

her husband, William de Fortibus, died and she returned to the shelter of the family home of Carisbrooke. Then, two years later in 1263, her brother, the Lord of the Castle, was treacherously poisoned while on a visit to his brother-in-law in Savoy. At the age of twenty-five the young widow found herself sole mistress of one of England's most powerful castles, in an essentially male and hostile world.

She survived and flourished and it was during her reign (for such it could be called) that there appeared the first clear accounts of the castle. She was a remarkably energetic and imaginative builder, so much so that her contemporaries took to referring to Carisbrooke as the 'new' castle. The building accounts give some idea of social conditions of the day and a few glimpses of Isabella's character. She was an innovator, one of the first in England to use glass for windows. She was religious and had a sense of style, to judge by the beautiful little chapel she constructed adjoining the great hall. She had a window seat built for herself in the north wall of her private chamber. It is still there, and many visitors climb the steps to sit there and look down the valley towards the village, as she must often have done. King Edward I purchased the castle from Isabella on the day she died and Carisbrooke was again in the hands of the monarch.

The castle experienced military action only twice: in 1136 it was besieged and taken by King Stephen; during the Hundred Years' War, in 1377, the French landed in strength on the north coast of the island, destroyed the towns of Yarmouth and Francheville and, advancing on Carisbrooke, besieged it. According to legend, the castle was saved by a bowman, Peter Heynoe.

'One Petrus de Heynoe came to sir Hugh Tyrell, then Captayne of the Island and told

△
Arms of the de Redvers family, rulers of the island 1100–1293

Vicar of Christchurch

Countess Isabella de Fortibus, last of the de Redvers ▷

Carisbrooke Castle Museum

△ *Engraving of the castle by George Brannon 1846*

him he woold undertake with his silver bowe to kill ye commander of ye French, taking his time, for he had observed him nyghtes and mornings he neare ye Castle which on leave he killed him owt of a loope hole on ye west syde of ye Castle. ❜

The death of their commander apparently demoralised the French who retreated to Yarmouth. An arrow slit still surviving *'on ye west syde of ye Castle'* has long been identified as 'Heynoe's loope.'

Scarcely had England emerged from the long struggle with the French when it was plunged into civil war with the Wars of the Roses. Caught up in a dynastic struggle, it was inevitable that the powerful men who controlled the castle would from time to time find themselves on the wrong side and so be convicted as traitors; three of the Captains of the Castle suffered this fate. Another inevitable result was the tightening of royal control. Never again would Carisbrooke pass into private hands, and after 1582 the once proud titles of Lord or Captain of the Castle was dropped; henceforward they would be known simply as governors.

The threat of the Spanish invasion brought Carisbrooke into the front line again in the 1580s. Queen Elizabeth I was aware that she was fighting not simply for her crown but for her life. If the enormous power of Spain, backed by the gold of the New World and the prayers of the Pope, should triumph over England, there would be little doubt about the fate of a 'heretic' queen. She appointed her cousin George Carey, second Lord

British Library

◁ *King Stephen from a fourteenth-century manuscript*

Hunsdon, as governor. The Queen could not have chosen a better man. Carey was thirty-four when he took up the post in 1582, with a distinguished political and military career behind him. But he was also very much a man of his time — that restless, inventive, imaginative period we call Elizabethan.

All over England, the old-fashioned homes of the nobility were being modernised and Carey followed suit, for unlike his immediate predecessors he spent much time at Carisbrooke and made it again fit for habitation. He not only adapted the great hall, but actually built an entire mansion next to it. He earned a reputation for lavish hospitality, frequently entertaining all the island gentry to splendid banquets.

'He was a most fine man in his housekeeping, and his meat was always served up to table with a concert of wind and still music.'

And neither were the servants forgotten:

◁ *Sir George Carey, Governor 1582 –1603*

'The laundry was never without a hogshead of wine and a cold pasty of venison for the maids.'

Replica of Carey's seal ▽

Carisbrooke Castle Museum

Carey vigorously set about improving the defences of the castle, willingly assisted by the islanders as fear and hatred of 'the Dons' was universal. The castle was in as bad a state of repair militarily as it had been domestically and the islanders contributed to its renovation

◁ *The keep towering above the great hall with the private apartments on the right*

Carisbrooke Castle Museum

Carisbrooke Castle in the sixteenth century

Model of the castle as it might have been in the fourteenth century

— the gentry sending materials, the ordinary people labouring. Some 3000 soldiers were quartered at Carisbrooke.

The Spanish Armada was sighted from the Isle of Wight on the morning of 26 July 1588. Carey later described in a letter to the Earl of Sussex how

> *'This morning began a great fight between both fleets . . . [which] were out of sight by three in the afternoon.'*

But though the Armada was defeated the threat from Spain remained and Carey insisted on the island being kept to a high state of readiness. Between 1597 and 1600 the parsimonious Queen Elizabeth was persuaded to spend money on Carisbrooke to extend and strengthen the defences because of renewed threat of Spanish invasion. Carey's were the last major alterations made to Carisbrooke.

The long royal association was broken during the Civil War when Parliament appointed the Earl of Pembroke as governor in place of the royalist Earl of Portland.

The castle continued to be kept in repair as a military defence until the eighteenth century but, apart from the period when it acted as the prison of

Bridgeman Art Library

Lord Pembroke, Governor 1642–47 painted by Van Dyck

Charles I, it played no further part in national history. By the early nineteenth century it was in a bad state of repair but was restored 'in a somewhat too liberal spirit,' according to a historian, in 1856. More and more the governors tended to live in comfortable quarters elsewhere but in 1896 Princess Beatrice, succeeding her husband as governor, restored the residential tradition even though she used the castle only as a summer residence. She died in 1944. In July 1965 Earl Mountbatten of Burma was ceremonially installed as Governor of Carisbrooke by Queen Elizabeth II.

Prince Henry and Princess Beatrice of Battenberg ▷

Princess Beatrice's initial from the outer gate ▷▷

Installation of Earl Mountbatten as Governor of Carisbrooke Castle by Queen Elizabeth II, July 1965 ▽

The great hall has been, for at least 800 years, the living heart of the castle. Decade after decade and century after century people made it their home and, as people always do, each new occupant set about adapting the building for his or her own purposes. It is therefore the most difficult of all the surviving sections of the castle to understand for century rubs shoulder with century. But it is also the most rewarding of all Carisbrooke's buildings for here one comes into contact with living history. Here, in an upper room in 1647–48, the royal prisoner, Charles, whiled away the dreary hours writing a justification for his actions. In a room nearby his little daughter Elizabeth later died of pneumonia. Here, in the late thirteenth century, the formidable Isabella de Fortibus held her state and here, in the early twentieth century, the scarcely less formidable Princess Beatrice, daughter of Queen Victoria, ruled as the last resident governor of the castle and the island.

The present building started life in the thirteenth century as a great gaunt stone building, open to the roof, without an upper floor, warmed by a fire in the middle, the smoke from which sometimes went through a hole in the roof, but just as often wreathed around the occupants. The hall was the social centre, not only of the castle but of the island.

The first domestic buildings were to the north of the hall (on the left as one enters the castle) followed by others to the south. A great improvement to the hall took place about 1400 when the captain, William de Montacute, inserted the handsome fireplace which even now dominates the ground floor. On the right of the fireplace one can still see the remains of a window, blocked up when the fireplace was inserted and rediscovered in the nineteenth century.

The next great period of change was in the sixteenth century under the energetic

Fireplace inserted into the great hall in the late fourteenth century

George Carey. It was he who built the porch to the hall and added the upper floor. But it was he, too, who brutally desecrated Isabella de Fortibus's chapel in the southeast corner of the hall. He needed to increase accommodation and so built an upper floor in the chapel, destroying its fine medieval detail. In the eighteenth century the present staircase was inserted; it is now the main access to the upper floor. The eighteenth-century builders panelled over the stone and the very existence of the chapel was forgotten until the restoration of 1856. Today the remains of the thirteenth-century vaulting and windows are plainly visible.

Halfway up the steps a door leads into the building called the Constable's Lodgings, rebuilt and extended by William de Montacute in the fourteenth century. It is now used as store rooms and lecture rooms and is not open to the public. Among them, probably the room now used as a schoolroom, is Charles I's bed chamber, from which he first attempted to escape. The entire block formed the suite of rooms once occupied by Princess Beatrice.

The great hall is now occupied by the Carisbrooke Castle Museum, with an interesting history in its own right. It is, in fact, an amalgamation of two museums, the Isle of Wight Museum, founded in Newport in the early nineteenth century, and Carisbrooke Castle Museum, founded as a memorial to Princess Beatrice's husband who died in 1896. It is administered quite separately from the castle under a trust, with the Princess personally appointing honorary curators, and was established at first in the upper rooms of the gatehouse. After the death of the Princess in 1944, King George VI gave permission for it to be housed in the great hall, which had hitherto been used as the governor's house.

◁ *Remains of the Chapel of St Peter built by Countess Isabella*

A sconce (candle holder) ▽

◁ *Thirteenth-century windows of the hall, blocked by the fireplace*

◁ *William de Montacute, Earl of Salisbury, Lord of the Island 1385 – 97*

The lord's private apartments, rebuilt and extended by William de Montacute, 1385 – 97

THE ROYAL PRISONER

Were it not for our knowledge of its tragic end there would be an element of farce about the captivity of Charles I at Carisbrooke. The swaggering Captain Burley, who made a clumsy attempt to rescue him; the King getting stuck in the bars of his window; his jailer's courteously ironic remark that he had come to pay his respects because he had heard the King was leaving — all this has a comic touch. There is also the irony that Charles voluntarily placed himself in Carisbrooke, to its unfortunate governor's dismay. This was the captivity that need never have happened.

In 1647 Charles was a prisoner in Hampton Court while his captors wrangled over what to do with him. In fear of his life he escaped, and it is by no means unlikely that Cromwell had a hand in the escape, for the Protector did not share the hatred that the more fanatical of his supporters had for the King. But where to go? To escape to the Continent would probably mean that he could never come back, whereas the Isle of Wight, though relatively remote, was part of his kingdom. And finally the then Governor of Carisbrooke, Colonel Hammond, though a Parliamentarian was the brother of the King's chaplain. Charles therefore put himself under Hammond's protection.

Poor Hammond was appalled; an

Charles I and Colonel Hammond, Governor of the Island

honourable soldier, torn between his duty to the King and to Parliament. As he later explained:

> *'I knew not what course to take; but upon serious consideration, weighing the great concernment that the person of the King is of, in this junction of affairs, to the settlement of the peace of the kingdom, I resolved it my duty to the King, to the Parliament, and kingdom, to use the utmost of my endeavours to preserve his person.'*

At first Charles was treated as an honoured guest, even free to ride around the island. But Captain Burley's ill-planned attempt at rescue, with a hardening of Parliament's attitude, forced Hammond to put the King under greater restraint. He did his best to make him comfortable, even turning the outer bailey into a bowling green for his recreation. But the King was then a

Carisbrooke Castle Museum

John Livesay's drawing showing the windows as they were in 1798. Charles I tried to escape through the lowest of the four windows

Captain John Burley

Window inserted in 1856 which replaced that through which Charles first tried to escape

prisoner, not a guest.

A second attempt at rescue on 20 March 1648 very nearly succeeded. The King was still lodged in the Constable's Lodgings adjoining the great hall and it was arranged that he would escape through the window, lower himself down by a cord, hasten across the courtyard to the curtain wall behind the chapel of St Nicholas. This could easily be ascended from inside and he would be lowered outside to where two men were waiting with a spare horse. Unfortunately the King had omitted to check whether he could get through the bars of the window; he could not, and the attempt was abandoned.

Another attempt at escape was planned for the night of 28 May, after Charles had been moved to a room in the north curtain wall (the window is now marked with a plaque). The King had been supplied with a quantity of nitric acid and with it he cut through one of the bars, making escape possible. But by that time too many people were in the plot, Hammond was informed and shortly before the time for the escape attempt the colonel came to the King's room:

'I am come to take leave of your majesty, for I hear you are going away.'

The King remained in this room until he was removed from Carisbrooke to Newport on 6 September and thence to

Window of King Charles's second bed chamber

Bowling green prepared for Charles I

Carisbrooke Castle Museum

▲ Princess Elizabeth, daughter of Charles I, on her deathbed, 8 September 1650

The National Trust

◁ *The children of Charles I: the future Prince Henry, Princess Elizabeth and Charles II*

London on 30 November. Charles I was executed in London at 11am on 30 January 1649.

There was a brief and poignant epilogue. The future Charles II had escaped but his little brother, Henry, Duke of Gloucester, and fourteen-year-old sister, Elizabeth, were in Parliament's hands. They were moved to Carisbrooke in August 1650 and were treated with every respect and consideration. But Princess Elizabeth, a delicate child already suffering from rickets, contracted pneumonia after being caught in a shower on the bowling green and was found dead in her room on the morning of 8 September. She is buried in Newport parish church, where Queen Victoria had a monument raised in her memory. The little boy, Henry, continued in his lonely captivity for nearly three years before being released to join his family abroad in 1653.

Head of Charles I's walking stick ▽

Carisbrooke Castle Museum

Charles I's ruby ring ▷

A medieval castle could hold out for an astonishingly long time on a starvation diet; if the water supply failed, however, it would be obliged to surrender within days. This, in fact, is exactly what happened at Carisbrooke in 1136 when King Stephen was besieging Baldwin de Redvers. Baldwin had to surrender when the water supply failed. It is possible that the only well at that time was that in the keep, for this has been known to fail many times. Certainly the Captain of the Castle decided to dig a more reliable well and, probably with the aid of dowsers, this was located in the courtyard, below the present wellhouse, where it descends 161ft (49m) through rock. It was in constant use for over six centuries, from the early twelfth century until the early twentieth century when the castle was

The wellhouse, built in the late sixteenth century

linked to the water main. It still contains water, about 40ft (12m) deep, which it is said Princess Beatrice liked to drink.

There has been a wellhouse over the well since 1291; the present structure dates from 1587. The first treadwheel also dates from 1291; it was repaired or rebuilt in 1334. The present wheel was installed during the reconstruction of 1587. It is probable that prisoners were first used to tread the wheel until a donkey was introduced in the eighteenth century. Until 1880 only one donkey was kept at the castle but the number was gradually increased and there are now four. Their training takes about seven months; they then work for about two hours a day for demonstration purposes.

The wellhouse is extremely popular but can accommodate only a few people at a time — hence the lengthy and frequent queues. If the opportunity presents itself to enter the wellhouse without queueing, it is advisable to do so, even if one has not reached that stage in the tour.

Treadwheel and winding mechanism, built in 1587 ▽

The castle donkeys ▽▽

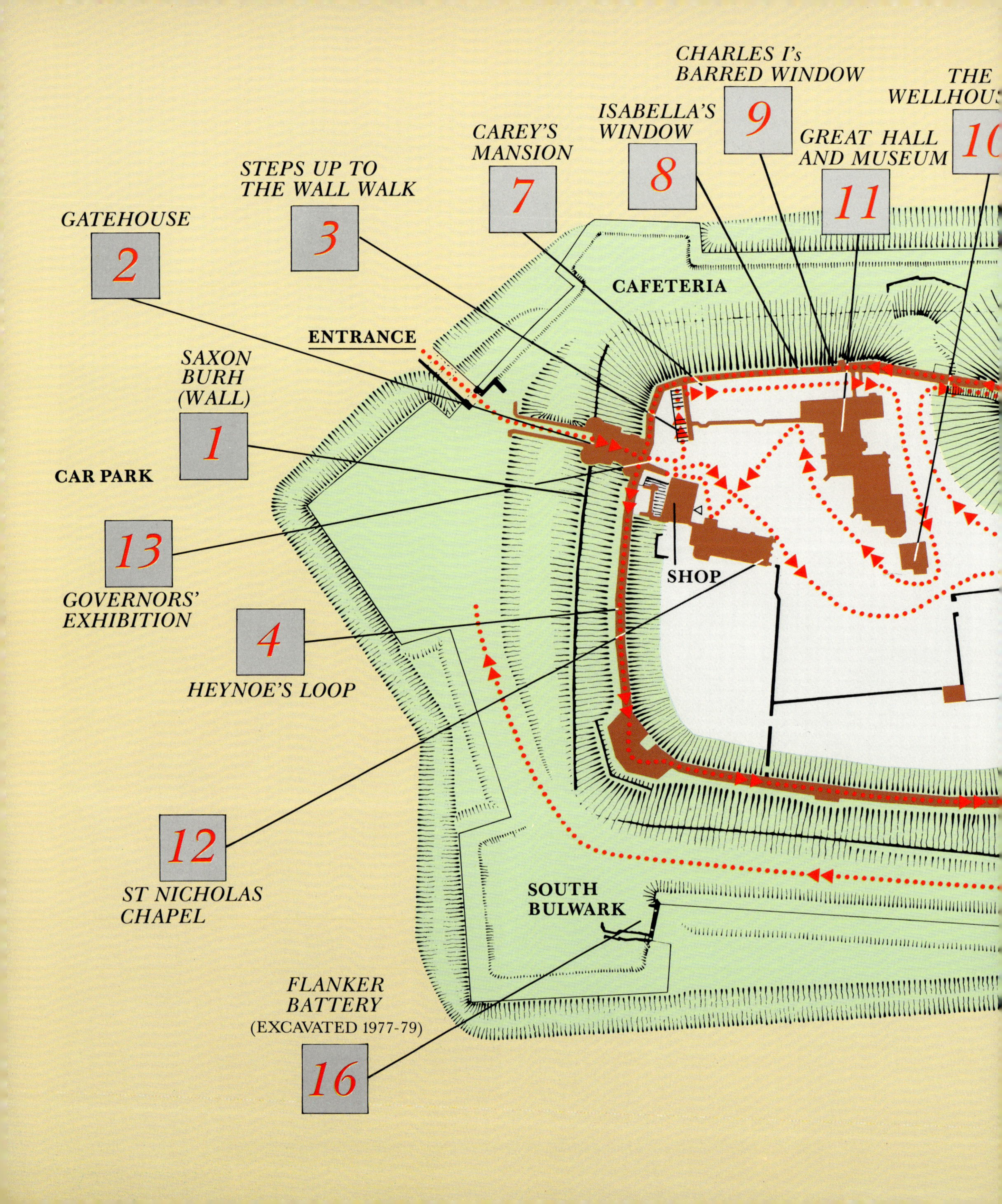

CHARLES I's BARRED WINDOW
9
THE WELLHOUS
10
ISABELLA'S WINDOW
8
GREAT HALL AND MUSEUM
11
CAREY'S MANSION
7
STEPS UP TO THE WALL WALK
3
GATEHOUSE
2
CAFETERIA
ENTRANCE
SAXON BURH (WALL)
1
CAR PARK
13
GOVERNORS' EXHIBITION
SHOP
4
HEYNOE'S LOOP
12
ST NICHOLAS CHAPEL
SOUTH BULWARK
FLANKER BATTERY
(EXCAVATED 1977-79)
16

TOUR OF THE CASTLE

The numbers on this plan incidate the places described in the text. By following this recommended route you will most easily see all the places of interest

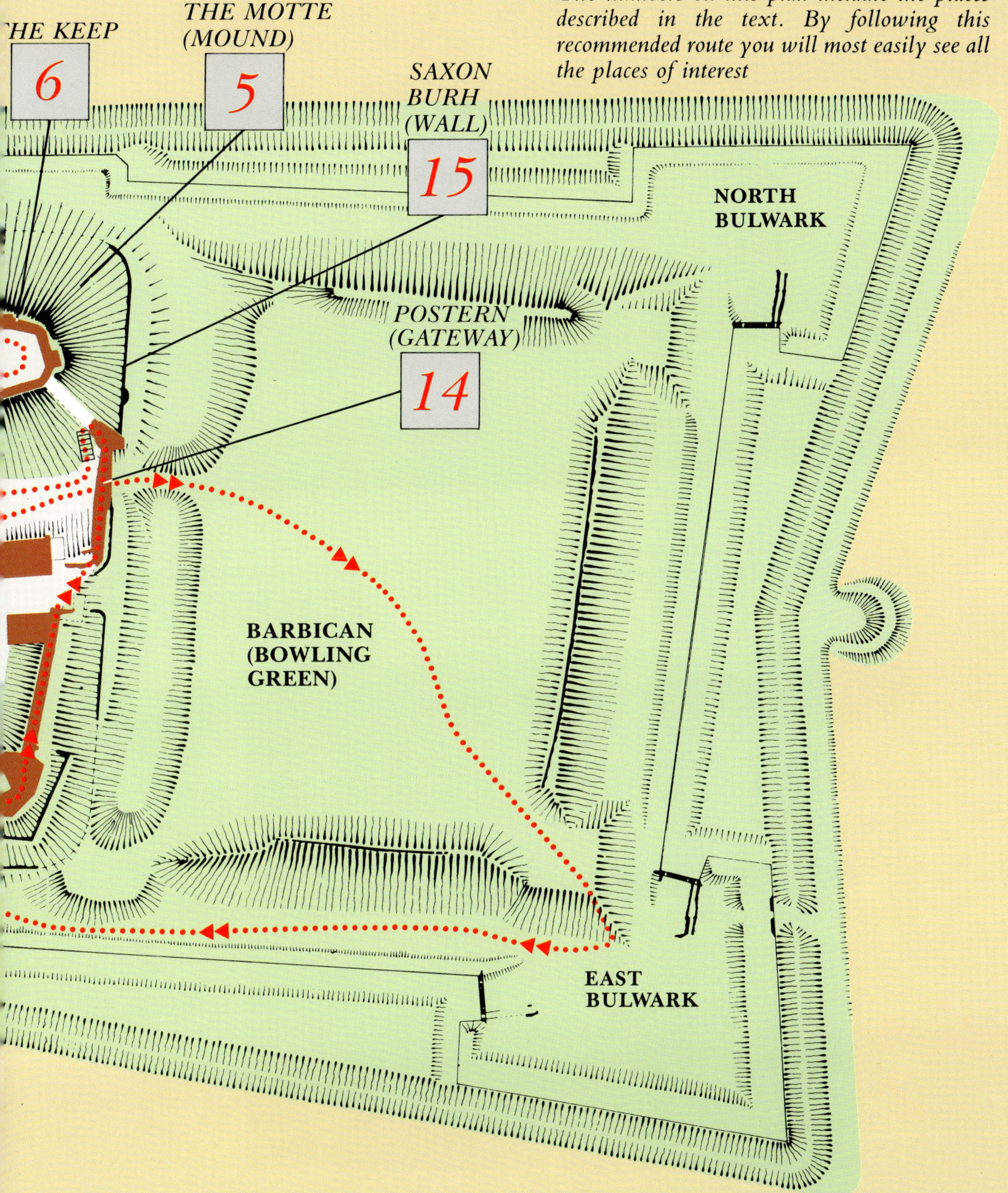

A full tour of the castle covers three main areas: a circuit of the Norman curtain walls, beginning with the entrance and gatehouse; the internal, domestic buildings; the outer bailey, including the sixteenth-century fortifications. Numbering is used in the following tour to identify important or interesting aspects (see the plan).

Gatehouse and walls

The entrance to Carisbrooke provides a virtually textbook illustration of a castle adapting itself to changing military conditions. A redbrick bridge leads over a ditch created as part of artillery defences and built between 1597 and 1600. The pediment over the gateway bears the initials of Elizabeth I and the date 1598. On the far side of the second ditch, however, can be seen the stone wall — now embedded in the mound — which formed part of the late Saxon *burh* [1]. The gatehouse [2] is a little castle in its own right and originally housed the gate guard. This, too, has been altered over the centuries. The front, with its drum towers, was built about 1335 in front of an earlier gateway, but the upper parts of the towers with their gunports and machicolations [openings in the floor through which missiles could be dropped onto assailants] over the gate are much later — probably about 1470. In the gateway itself one can see traces of three consecutive portcullis grooves, the position of each showing the growth of the gateway. The wooden doors are modern.

Turn left on passing through the gateway, ascend the steps [3] and turn left on to the wall walk. This southern circuit of the curtain walls may be historically less important than the northern, but it is perhaps even more beautiful for the wall walk passes by the branches of great trees, with excellent views of the domestic buildings within the castle and the sixteenth-century exterior fortifications. On the right, immediately

past the gatehouse roof, look for an arrow slit [4]. This may be 'Heynoe's loop' and it is a good example of the kind of slit used by bowmen, unlike some which were altered for use by cannon. Continue past the two corner towers which were strengthened to take cannon in the sixteenth century. These towers are known as 'knights' and were built around the outer face of the original Norman towers.

Keep

Descend to ground level by the steps on the motte [mound] [5]. Keep the motte to the right. This provides an excellent close-up view of the mound which Richard de Redvers' workers threw up shortly after 1100, laboriously working with wooden shovels and wicker baskets. Children love counting the steps up to the keep but usually get the number wrong. There are seventy-one.

The walls of the keep [6] are perhaps lower than when they were built shortly before 1136. A castle keep was never a

△ *Interior of the keep, showing fourteenth-century gatehouse and sixteenth-century internal walls added to the Norman shell keep*

◁ *Interior of the gate passage, built in the thirteenth century and extended c1335*

◁ *Loophole for use by bowmen*

Norman shell keep, built before 1136. The gatehouse was added c1335

comfortable place in which to live and it would have been abandoned when its military use was ended. The gateway was built about 1335 and one can still see the portcullis groove in the outside arch. The walls inside the keep are part of the sixteenth-century modification but there is a fourteenth-century garderobe [latrine] recessed into the outer wall. Also in the keep is the first well dug in the castle. It goes down 160ft (49m) and the impressions of the timber support of the windlass can be seen in the near-by wall.

Domestic buildings

After exploring the keep (the upper walls provide a superb view over the whole castle) descend the steps, not to ground level but to the wall walk, and continue towards the start of the tour. Stop to look down into the ruins of George Carey's mansion [7]. This was a two-storey house with two bay windows looking into the courtyard. The shape of their foundations can still be seen, with the remains of a chimney in the far (eastern) wall. Descend to the path running along at first-floor level within this mansion and double back below the wall walk into the ruins of the earliest domestic quarters of the castle, so placed that in times of emergency the occupants could escape up into the keep. Isabella de Fortibus's window [8] in her great chamber was probably the first to be glazed in the castle. To the left of the window are the remains of an oven and chimney built in

△ *Medieval well in the keep*

◁ *Fourteenth-century garderobe (latrine) in the keep*

◁ *Domestic buildings: Carey's mansion is on the left, Isabella's great hall on the right*

what became known as Carey's Kitchen, an excellent example of how one generation after another adapted the building. To the right and above can be seen the barred window 9 of the last place of captivity of Charles I.

Continue on down into the courtyard and on to the wellhouse 10, the great hall and museum 11. Next visit St Nicholas Chapel 12.

The chapel is the work of Percy Stone, the nineteenth-century island architect and historian of Carisbrooke Castle. There has been a chapel on the site since 1070 but it was demolished and rebuilt at least twice and was a roofless ruin in the nineteenth century. In 1904 it was decided to rebuild the chapel completely, to mark the 250th anniversary of the execution of Charles I, and have the bust of Charles I by Bernini, bearing the single word REMEMBER, placed in it. The organ is from the Rolls Chapel in Chancery Lane and was presented by Edward VII. The statues around the altar represent the patron saints of all the island's churches and the woodwork is from HMS *Nettle*, one of the last of the wooden warships. Princess Beatrice commissioned the altar painting in memory of her son, Maurice, killed at Ypres in 1914.

Later it was decided that the entire chapel should become the memorial for all those of the Isle of Wight who were killed in the First and Second World Wars. The names of two thousand men are inscribed on the wall panels.

The Governors' Exhibition 13 is a collection of portraits and biographies of the Captains and Governors of Carisbrooke made at the request of Earl Mountbatten.

◁ *Window of Countess Isabella's chamber*

The ruined chapel before it was rebuilt by Percy Stone ▷

Carisbrooke Castle Museum

◁ *Fireplace and oven from Carey's conversion of Isabella's room to a kitchen*

Bust of Charles I by Bernini ▷

Chapel organ presented by Edward VII ▷

Outer bailey

Visitors tend to overlook the outer bailey for its access is somewhat hidden. This is a pity as the area outside the curtain walls is extremely beautiful — especially in spring with masses of cowslips and primroses — and recent archaeological investigations have thrown light on the defences constructed at the time of the Spanish threat.

On the south side of the motte is a narrow gateway or postern 14 in the curtain wall. The gateway looks like an afterthought, and that is exactly what it is, pierced through the wall to allow access to the fortifications built in the sixteenth century. Immediately ahead is the bowling green which Colonel Hammond constructed for the recreation of Charles I, on the site of the old *place d'armes* — the place where military exercises and perhaps tournaments would have taken place. From the centre look back at the castle. The bowling green occupies the original undisturbed surface of the hill. The Saxon builders evidently decided that the entire crest of the hill was too big to enclose and so built a wall across, in effect dividing it into two. The base of the wall 15, facing one when looking back at the castle from the bowling green, is formed of the original Saxon *burh* (the line of stones to the left and right of the postern gate is Saxon, corresponding to the similar line at the entrance on the western side of the castle). The Normans simply built on top.

◁ Statues of saints in the sanctuary of the chapel